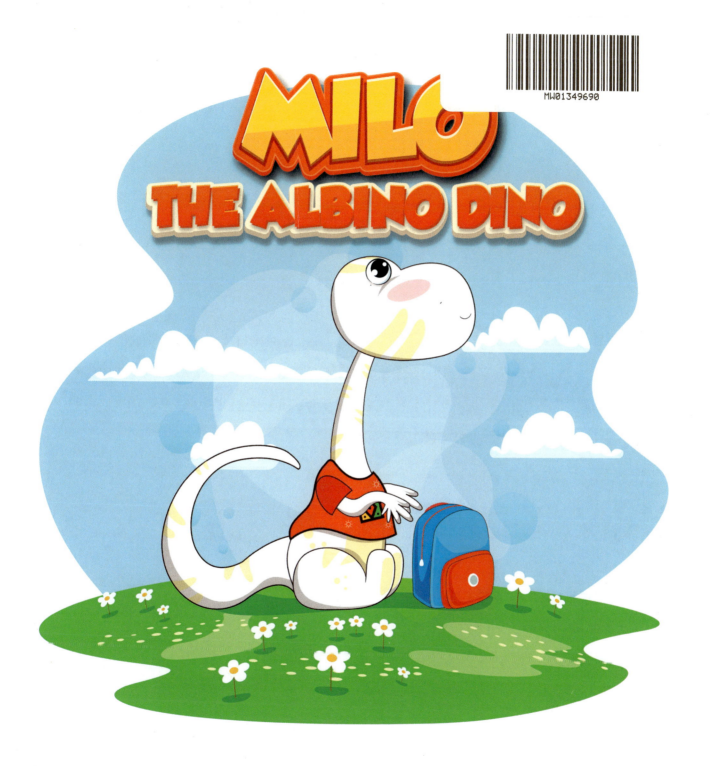

Copyright 2021 © Squeedeal Publishing.

All rights reserved. No part of this book may be reproduced in any manner – without the express written consent of the publisher, except in the case of brief excerpts in critical reviews and articles. All inquiries should be addressed to:

Squeedeal LLC
3201 Edwards Mill Rd #140 Raleigh, NC 27612
or
support@squeedeal.com
www.squeedeal.com/squeedeal-publishing
ISBN: 978-1-7347738-1-1

While you might think he comes from Mississippi, he actually comes from South Africa.

Milo is not a regular dinosaur. He was born an albino.

That means his skin is white and sensitive to the sun, so he has to put on a lot of sunscreen.

Or when he walks into a candy store.

Milo was never picked for soccer. Never asked to play checkers or hide-and-seek.

The other kids thought that he was different, so they really did not want to play with him.

"I'm sure you will have a great time together because you are more alike."

Another **albino** dino?

Milo never thought about that possibility! Another dino like him...

"He must feel as alone as I do," he thought.

"I must find him!"

The next day Milo hung a poster on the board at school.

"What is that?"

asked Bobbie the Bagaceratops.

Bobbie got excited. "I thought you were the only one!" he shouted.

"My older brother said that there are no two dinos that are alike. If there is another one like you, then I can prove my brother is wrong."

"And he said he will get me a comet-shaped lollipop if I do".

Bobbie decided to help Milo in his quest and called his friends to help.

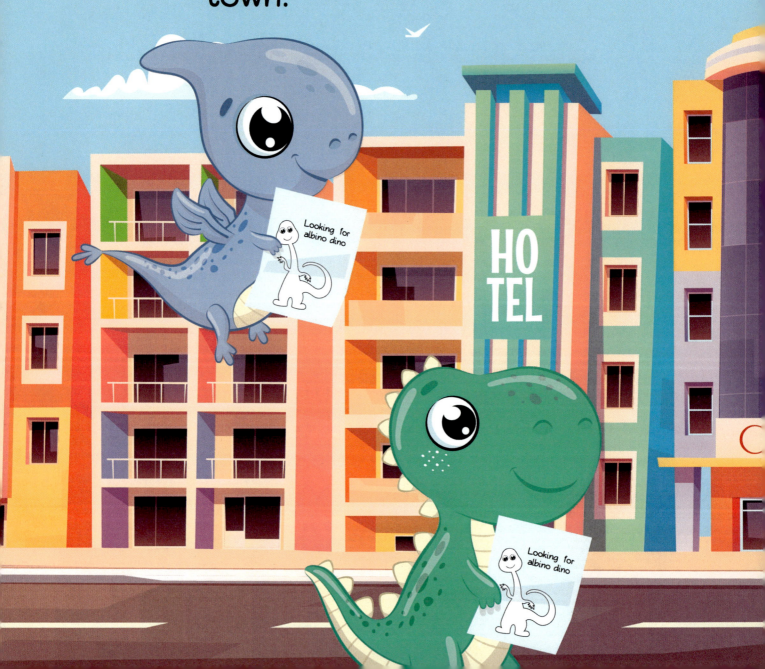

First, they made signs and hung them around town.

Then, they rode their bicycles around the neighborhood, searching every house and corner.

Because his bones are hollow, he was able to pedal much faster, so he connected all of the bicycles to his and pulled everyone up the hill.

After that, they climbed onto the trees to look as far as the eye could see.

Because of his long and strong neck, Milo helped his friends to climb up into the treetops.

Looking for albino dino

They searched all over—in the air,

on land,

Looking albino

and even under the sea. But there was no other albino dino to be found.

After days of searching the group was tired and ready to give up their search.

"Hey Milo," said Bobbie.

"I'm sorry that you were not able to find another albino dino, but it was really fun hanging out with you".

"I don't have to go home yet".

"Want to play soccer?"

Milo gave a big smile and said yes. They all went to the soccer field

and played until their moms came over to see why everyone was late for dinner.

For the first time ever, Milo felt that he was just the same as everyone else. Even better, others saw his qualities and wanted him around.

He helped Bobbie hang a poster in his room.

He helped Mike get his drone that was stuck in a treetop.

He also helped Matt practice for the national dino-run marathon.

Through their journey, they realized that while Milo might look different, he was actually just like any other dinosaur.

And more importantly, he was a really good friend.

Hello, Squeedly friend! I hope you enjoyed this book! I'm sure you probably have more questions from what we just read, so I decided to add a few more fun facts for you:

- The country of South Africa is a peninsula, which means that it's surrounded by water on three of its sides. So it's almost like an island, only on one part it's connected to the rest of the continent. **Do you know which continent it's connected to? And, can you think of another peninsula?**

- Speaking of South Africa, do you know that this country has **eleven official languages: isiZulu, isiXhosa, Afrikaans, Sepedi, Setswana, English, Sesotho, Xitsonga, siSwati, Tshivenda, and isiNdebele. Other notable languages include Khoi, Nama, and San. What languages do you or your family speak?**

- The Massospondylus had a herbivorous and omnivorous lifestyle. That means that this dinosaur ate both vegetables and meat. **What animals do you know that enjoy the same lifestyle?**

- Dinosaurs like the Massospondylus hatched from eggs. Yes, just like chicks! **What other animals hatch from an egg?**

- Albinism is a very rare disorder and is estimated that only 1 in 20,000 people are born with it. It causes impaired vision (it's harder for them to see clearly) and very sensitive skin (they get burned really fast from the sunlight). **Can you think of other disorders that people might be born with?**

- Human beings, plants, and animals can have albinism. **Have you seen an albino animal before? If not, you can search for albino animals on the internet.**

If you liked the book, please write a quick review on Amazon or Goodreads so we can find more Squeedly friends like you. Thank you for reading this story with me, and please visit again soon!

Amazon

Goodreads

For more Squeedly and Friends books,
check out Far Beyond the Sun

Thank you.

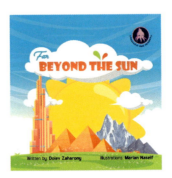

Amazon

Made in the USA
Columbia, SC
07 May 2021